The AQUARIUM
TAKE~ALONG BOOK

••

by SHELDON L. GERSTENFELD V.M.D.
illustrated by PAUL HARVEY

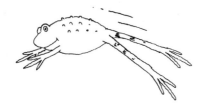

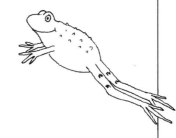

VIKING

For Traudi and Tyler

Writing a book about aquariums is like playing the piano.
You have to know the scales and how to play a tuna.

—Sheldon L. Gerstenfeld, V.M.D.

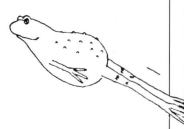

VIKING
Published by the Penguin Group
Penguin Books USA Inc., 375 Hudson Street, New York, New York 10014, U.S.A.
Penguin Books Ltd, 27 Wrights Lane, London W8 5TZ, England
Penguin Books Australia Ltd, Ringwood, Victoria, Australia
Penguin Books Canada Ltd, 10 Alcorn Avenue, Toronto, Ontario, Canada M4V 3B2
Penguin Books (N.Z.) Ltd, 182–190 Wairau Road, Auckland 10, New Zealand

Penguin Books Ltd, Registered Offices: Harmondsworth, Middlesex, England
First published in 1994 by Viking, a division of Penguin Books USA Inc.

10 9 8 7 6 5 4 3 2 1

Text copyright © Sheldon L. Gerstenfeld, 1994
Illustrations copyright © Paul Harvey, 1994
All rights reserved

LIBRARY OF CONGRESS CATALOGING-IN-PUBLICATION DATA
Gerstenfeld, Sheldon L.,
The aquarium take-along-book / by Sheldon L. Gerstenfeld ;
illustrated by Paul Harvey.   p. cm.
Summary: A guide to the natural environments, skills, and adaptations of water animals plus
information about preserving marine life.
ISBN 0-670-84386-5
1. Aquatic animals—Juvenile literature. 2. Animals—Juvenile literature. [1. Aquatic animals.]
I. Harvey, Paul, ill. II. Title.
QL120.G47 1994   591.92—dc20   93-23059 CIP AC

Printed in U.S.A.   Set in 12 pt. New Century Schoolbook

Contents

About This Book

We must be kind to our water world. It is the only one that we have, and it can never be replaced. The earth has existed for two billion years. Humans have been here for only a short time. In the last one hundred years we have done more damage to the earth than has occurred in all the rest of time.

We can help save our water world by getting to know more about what it's like. We see the creatures that live there most often when they come near the borders of our land world. But many of their secrets and surprises are hidden beneath the water's surface. Fortunately, we don't need scuba-diving gear to visit the water world. The aquarium is a good place to see its inhabitants at home, without getting wet.

This book tells about the creatures you might see in an aquarium and lets you in on some of the behind-the-scenes secrets of the aquarium's scientists, veterinarians, and keepers. When you have the chance to go to an aquarium yourself, you can take *The Aquarium Take-Along Book* with you. And if you can't visit one right now, consider the book your own private aquarium as you start exploring our wonderful water world.

There are many who are trying to reverse the process of its destruction—to heal our blue jewel of the universe. Among those who have influenced my life and the writing of this book are: Donna Place, Fred Nichy, and Dave Radosh of the Fisheries Aquarium in Woods Hole, Massachusetts; Captain Nicholas Brown and Carey Rowsom of the National Aquarium in Baltimore, Maryland; Dr. Bob Bullis and Dr. John Valois of the Marine Biological Laboratory in Wood Hole and the University of Pennsylvania; Bruce Miller, General Curator of Aquatic Systems at the Living Sea in Lake Buena Vista, Florida; Erica Ramus of *Reptile and Amphibian Magazine*; Roland Anderson and C. J. Carson of the Seattle Aquarium; Janet Pascal; Dr. John Gratzek and Dr. Donald Abt, who made AquaVet such an exciting program for me; and Karen Warneck my veterinary technician.

My dear son, Tyler, is my best teacher. I know that there is a future for the earth with his guiding light.

—S. L. G.

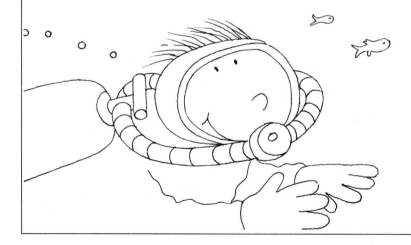

THE AQUARIUM TAKE-ALONG BOOK

Bony Fish

There are almost 20,000 known species of bony fish—those with a skeleton made of bone. Sharks and rays are not bony fish. They have a skeleton made of cartilage—a softer and more flexible material. Both kinds of fish are designed to balance and move through water with the help of fins. They breathe by getting oxygen from the water passing over their gills. Each species of fish has a special shape, set of body parts, and color pattern that help it survive in its water world.

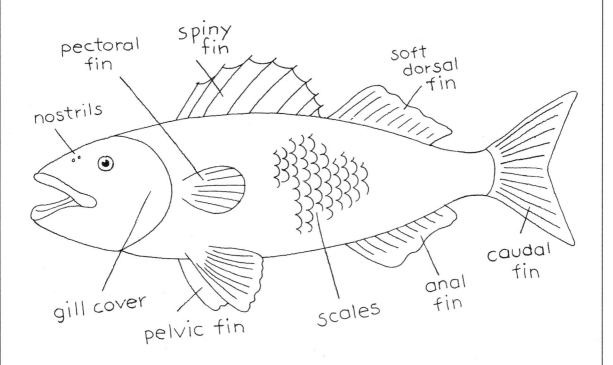

Looking at Fish

M O U T H

The location and shape of the mouth will show you how the fish gathers its food. Bottom feeders usually have mouths that face the bottom. This is also true of the non-bony fish. For example, the ray's mouth is on the bottom. The ray swoops over its food and sucks it into its mouth, where it is crushed by powerful grinding plates. A midwater feeder has a mouth at the tip of its snout. A top feeder has an upturned, scooplike mouth for eating floating insects.

B O D Y   S H A P E

Along with the mouth, body shape will give you clues to the fish's lifestyle. A surface-loving fish is flat on top, rather than high and rounded. This allows the fish to swim close to the surface and not be seen by a predator and become a potential meal. Disc-shaped, flattened fish usually live in slow-moving waters, while those shaped like a cylinder live in fast-moving waters. Bottom dwellers have flat bellies so that they can hug the bottom. Mud-burrowing fish tend to be wormlike.

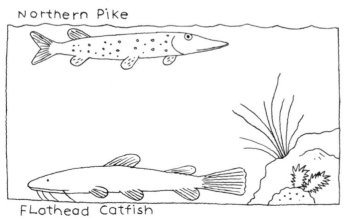

Northern Pike

Flathead Catfish

SKIN

In most cases, bony fish are covered with a layer of overlapping plates called scales. The scales are covered with a thin layer of slimy mucus that protects against parasites and contains antibodies to fight off infection.

FINS

Fins are used for moving, steering, and balance. The *dorsal* (top) and *anal* (bottom) fins act just like the keel (deep underpart) of a boat and keep the fish from rolling. The tail fin is the "power" fin. The *pectoral*, or "arm," fins are used for steering.

The lionfish has fins with long, hollow spines that contain venom. If another kind of fish touches a lionfish, he's "fin"-ished.

EYES

Most fish, unlike humans, have eyes on either side of the head. Fish get two separate views of the world around them. Flounders— "flat as a pancake" fish—are exceptions. Their two eyes are together on top. This helps them to see what is going on even when they are hiding on the sea bottom. Rays' eyes are also both on top.

Fish see in color. They have no eyelids and do not blink. Saltwater does not burn their eyes. Tears are not necessary, since their eyes are always kept moist with water.

The Tale of the Tail

The shape of the tail often tells you the swimming habits of the fish. Continuous, high-speed swimmers usually have crescent or forked caudal (tail) fins. Those with truncated square-ended tail fins are usually slow movers, but they can make a few fast dashes.

water out

Gill Skills

Fish breathe by forcing water over their featherlike gills. Oxygen that is dissolved in the water is absorbed into the bloodstream across the delicate gill membranes. Carbon dioxide is expelled. Ammonia, a chemical that is handled by the kidneys in humans, is excreted in large amounts by the gills. Watch the gill flaps move on the side of a fish.

Hearing Something Fishy

Fish would look pretty silly with earlobes. They don't need them. Humans have them to capture sound waves and direct them to a fluid-filled area inside their ears. We don't hear the sounds until the wave is transferred to the liquid. Fish are already in the water, so they get their sound waves ready-to-use. You can try hearing like a fish by hitting two rocks together when you are under water. The sound will seem to be coming from all directions at once, because the whole pool is sending your ear sound waves it can use. Fish do not need an ear canal, but they do have the inner ear structures that send sounds to the brain. Fish also detect sound through their gas-filled swim bladder and a line of nerves, called the lateral line, present in "portholes" running along the length of the fish.

Sniff, Snaffle, Snuffle

Fish have 2–4 nostril openings on the front of the snout. The openings do not lead into breathing chambers, as in humans, but directly to the smelling center. Chemicals and smells travel well in water.

The Water Balloon

Most bony fish, except a few bottom dwellers, have a gas-filled balloonlike organ, called a swim bladder. By letting gas in or out of its swim bladder, a fish can maintain a level position in the water or float up and down at will.

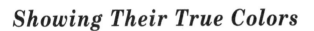

swim bladder

Showing Their True Colors

Many marine (sea) fish have colors that help them blend in with their environment. The color and markings of a flounder can change to match the sandy bottom. Some fish have stripes and spots that disguise their eyes, body shape, and size. The butterfly fish has a dark spot on its tail that looks like a big eye. It gives the fish a "head start" if it is attacked.

This Is My Territory

Some fish protect their territory more than other fish; some even chase away fish larger than themselves. The damselfish is very protective of its algae gardens on coral reefs.

Ouch!

Some fish have sharp, venomous spines on the back. The lionfish, the spotted scorpion fish, and the stonefish are three characters you don't want to bother.

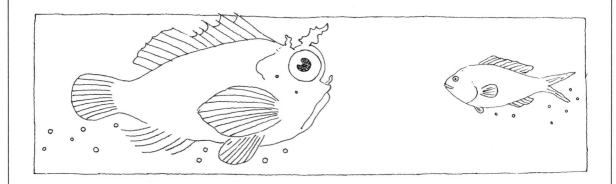

"Puff the Magic Dragon"—Oops, Fish

Some fish, like the puffer and the porcupine fish, protect themselves by inflating their bodies when they are threatened. They become too big to be swallowed by many predators, and too ugly and threatening to be eaten.

Going to School

Many fish stay in groups, called *schools*. Other fish swim alone or with a partner. Schooling gives the group many more eyes and ears to find food and to escape predators, and a place to meet potential mates.

Veterinarians'
BEHIND-THE-SCENES INFO

- Fish swim, drink, breathe, eat, eliminate their wastes, and mate in their room of water. The aquarium water quality is tested many times a day to make sure that it is healthy for fish. You should make the same tests on your home aquarium. Check with a veterinarian with a special interest in fish.

- Soft nets are used if a fish needs to be handled.

- Vaccines can protect fish from some diseases. They are given by injection or in food, or placed in the water and taken up by the gills.

- If surgery is necessary, an anesthetic is put in the water.

- Marine fish are very active and must be fed 2–4 times a day.

- New fish are isolated from the the main aquarium for 14–21 days to make sure that they do not have infections or parasites. They are usually given a dose of preventive medication in a bath, in their food, or by injection.

- The fish are watched for signs of illness: skin ulcers or white spots, color changes, frayed fins, fast or hard breathing, behavior changes (sitting on the bottom, rubbing the body on objects, not eating).

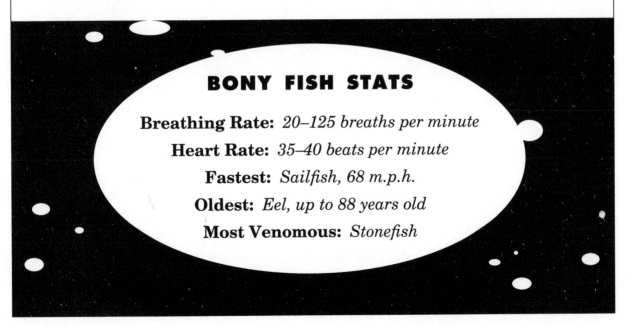

BONY FISH STATS

Breathing Rate: *20–125 breaths per minute*

Heart Rate: *35–40 beats per minute*

Fastest: *Sailfish, 68 m.p.h.*

Oldest: *Eel, up to 88 years old*

Most Venomous: *Stonefish*

Sharks

The dinosaurs roamed the earth 200 million years ago.
Humans have been on the earth for only a speck of time—
1 million years. Sharks are very good at their job.
That's why they have been around
for 400 million years!

Great
White
Shark

Looking at Sharks

TEETH

Sharks = *teeth!* A shark's jaw is lined with many rows of teeth so sharp that you could shave with them. The teeth are loosely attached in the jaw. As the front teeth are lost, other teeth move forward, ready to take their place. A young shark may replace a whole set of choppers every week. Some sharks will grow, use, and lose over 2,000 teeth in a year. Different types of sharks have different teeth shapes.

SKIN

Sharks are not huggable. Their sandpaperlike skin has sharp, tiny scales—called *denticles*— all over.

TAIL

Sharks are built for speed. They move the tail from side to side to drive themselves through the water at up to 20 miles per hour. The pectoral (left and right) fins behind the head work like airplane wings to help the shark glide.

Everybody Likes to Have a Friend—Even Sharks

A fish called the remora is the shark's friend. It attaches its sucker disc to the shark, rides along, and picks off parasites—keeping the shark clean. The shark thanks its friend by leaving scraps of food for it. This relationship, where two animals live together and help each other, is called *symbiosis*. Small, striped pilot fish swim close to sharks and pick up food scraps, but they don't help the shark in any observable way. The shark does not eat the pilot fish, nor will any other fish. It pays to stick close to your friend if you are a pilot fish.

Smell

Sharks have been called "swimming noses" because they can smell a drop of blood a quarter mile away. The direction of the smell is sensed by turning the head from side to side. Smell is so important to a shark's existence that almost 70 percent of its brain is used for the sense of smell.

Feeling Like a Shark

Here's how you would experience the world if you were born with the shark's special features:

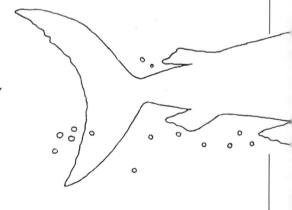

- You would be able to detect someone moving or breathing near you by picking up electrical impulses. You would have hundreds of holes above your lip that would contain organs called the *ampullae of Lorenzini*, which pick up electrical impulses.

- With your sensitive ears, you would be able to hear sounds in the water that are over 1/2 mile away.

- If the water was murky or dark, small openings on the sides of your body, containing the lateral line organs, would pick up vibrations from small movements in the water.

- Special pores on the side of your snout would pick up electrical impulses produced by the muscles of a hunted animal.

- You would be able to detect one drop of blood in 100,000 gallons of water.

Eating Like a Shark

- The shark's normal diet consists of fish. Big sharks also like sea lions and otters.

- Other things that sharks have eaten: crocodiles, horses, cows, dogs, cats, alarm clocks, bicycles, ship propellers, and torpedoes.

- Anything that is in the water is fair game when the shark is hungry.

- Sharks don't eat very often. In fact, some sharks eat once a month. The shark's liver is very large—25 percent of its weight. The liver is full of fat, which can be changed into body fuel between those "big snack attacks."

The Parade of Sharks

There are more than 350 types of sharks. Most are harmless to humans. In fact, fewer than 12 of the bigger sharks are considered dangerous. There are only about 30 shark attacks yearly, but millions of yellow-jacket attacks!

- The great white shark can be over 20 feet long. It has a nasty disposition, and has attacked more people than any other shark. It can eat a whole horse.

- Tiger sharks can be over 17 feet long. Just like the great whites, they are not known for their nice personality. A tiger shark can have 40 babies, called pups. Each pup is born about 2 feet long— longer than a full-grown house cat.

- Hammerhead sharks, 3–15 feet long, have a head shaped more like an airplane wing than a hammer; the eyes and nostrils are on the tip of the "wing." Considered to be dangerous to humans, these sharks normally like to eat stingrays. They use the special pores in their face to pick up the weak electrical currents produced by a stingray buried in the sand.

- Bull sharks are commonly reported in shark attacks on humans, since they swim close to shore, in shallow water, in search of food.

The nice, harmless basking and whale sharks are the largest sharks. Basking sharks are 30 feet long; whale sharks are 50–60 feet long—longer than two school buses end to end. These two kinds of sharks feed on *plankton*—tiny plants and animals that are filtered through "gill brushes," called gill rakers.

Veterinarians' BEHIND-THE-SCENES INFO

- Sharks are given medication, if needed, by injection or by hiding the medication in a fish.

- Since sharks may eat only once a week or even less frequently, medicine, when needed, can be injected daily with a pole syringe.

- Sharks and rays do not have gill flaps, just gill slits. Most cannot pump water over their gills. They must swim constantly to make water stream past their gills so they can breathe. Hourglass-shaped tanks with turnarounds give the sharks a long glide path for resting and breathing without using a lot of energy.

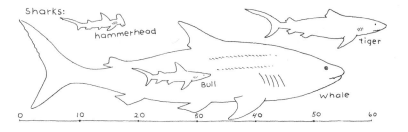

SHARK STATS

Longest: *Whale shark, 50 feet*

Smallest: *Dwarf shark, 4 inches*

Heaviest: *Whale shark, 40,000 pounds*

Rays

Rays are flattened sharks. The skeleton is made of cartilage, just like that of sharks. Rays swim so gracefully that they are sometimes called "birds of the sea." Their pectoral fins look like bird wings and make it possible for the ray to glide swiftly and gracefully. As the fins flap, they help dislodge food from the sandy bottom for bottom-feeding fish.

Looking at Rays

E Y E S

The ray's eyes are on top of its body, like eyes on a pancake—so it never sees the food that it eats.

M O U T H

The mouth is on the bottom. The ray swoops over the food and sucks it into its mouth, [where it is crushed by powerful grinding plates.]

F I N S

The large pectoral fins look like bird wings and make it possible for rays to glide swiftly and gracefully. The flapping fins also help dislodge food from the sandy bottom.

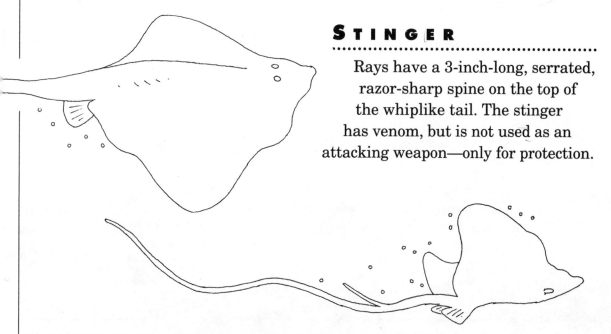

S T I N G E R

Rays have a 3-inch-long, serrated, razor-sharp spine on the top of the whiplike tail. The stinger has venom, but is not used as an attacking weapon—only for protection.

Ray Stings

In general, rays do not harm humans while they are swimming. If stepped on in sandy bottoms, they may sting. The wound is painful and slow to heal. Experienced swimmers and waders avoid stepping on rays by shuffling their feet. When a ray is nudged by a foot, it swims away.

Seafood Dinner

Shrimp, snails, crabs, clams, oysters, worms, and small fish are ray meals. Squid is the ray's favorite food.

The Ray Rest Stop

Rays like to lie buried on sandy sea floors.

Veterinarians'
BEHIND-THE-SCENES INFO

- For safety, the barbs are occasionally removed in the aquarium setting. They grow again.

- Medication can be placed in their favorite food, squid.

J·E·L·L·Y·F·I·S·H

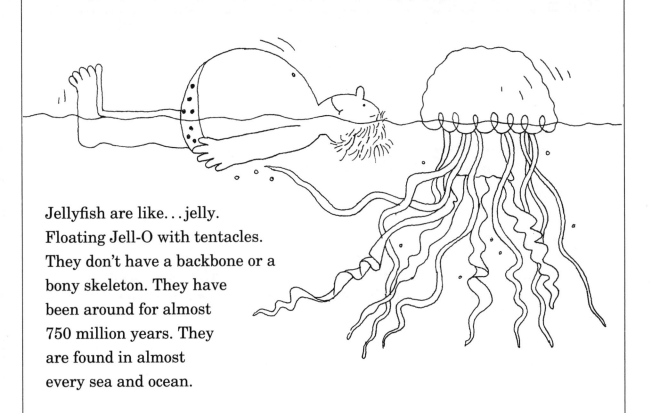

Jellyfish are like…jelly.
Floating Jell-O with tentacles.
They don't have a backbone or a
bony skeleton. They have
been around for almost
750 million years. They
are found in almost
every sea and ocean.

Looking at Jellyfish

B O D Y

Jellyfish have the shape of a bell, helmet, or umbrella. They float in currents but can also shoot upward, by pushing water out of the body with the help of muscles. They are more than a bowlful of jelly.

M O U T H

The mouth is surrounded by stinging tentacles. Do jellyfish give each other shocking kisses?

T E N T A C L E S

The tentacles inject a venom that paralyzes the prey. The tentacles have chemical receptors, which tell the jellyfish what is happening in the "neighborhood."

A R M S

The arms guide the meal to the mouth.

Stinging Like a Bee

- Most jellyfish stings will just cause some pain, swelling, and redness.

- The most dangerous, the sea wasp's, can kill a human in 1–5 minutes. The venom affects the heart.

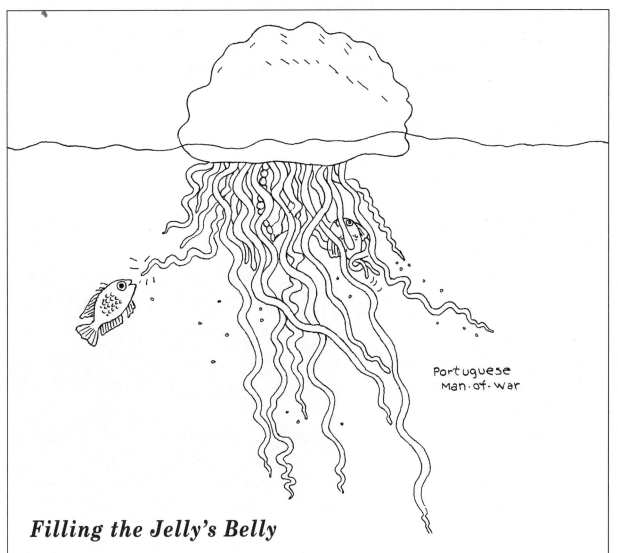

Portuguese
Man-of-war

Filling the Jelly's Belly

Jellyfish eat the small animals called *zooplankton* that drift in the water. They also eat some fish, which they sting with their tentacles.

Jellyfish as Snacks

Sea snails, turtles, and some fish like to eat jellyfish.

Veterinarians'
BEHIND-THE-SCENES INFO

- Jellyfish are kept in circular tanks or in tanks with rounded edges so that the water is constantly moving. Jellyfish depend on currents for horizontal movement.

- Jellyfish shrink if they don't eat.

- In the aquarium, they are fed young brine shrimp.

- If jellyfish touch one another, they don't get stung. They seem to recognize their "own kind" and thus do not sting members of their own species.

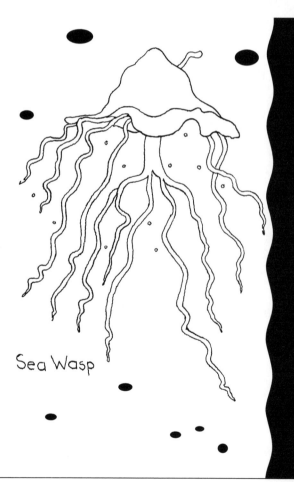

Sea Wasp

JELLYFISH STATS

Biggest Jellyfish:
Arctic jellyfish, 7 feet 6 inches, bell shaped

Longest Tentacles:
Arctic jellyfish, 120-foot tentacles

Most Lethal:
Sea wasp—a human's heart will stop beating in 5 minutes if he or she is stung by a sea wasp. The sea wasp is found from Indonesia to northern Australia.

CLAMS · AND · OYSTERS

Picture yourself as a clam or an oyster. Your foot would be near your mouth, your stomach would be above your mouth, and your intestines would pass through your heart. While this anatomical arrangement would not work well for humans, clams and oysters are as "happy as a clam" with it.

Clams and oysters are not crowd pleasers like penguins, whales, and seals, but they have a quiet dignity and offer "pearls of wisdom" on how to survive in the sea environment.

Clams and oysters are members of a large group of shelled creatures called *mollusks*. There are over 75,000 species of mollusks, including snails, squid, and octopuses. Not all mollusks live in the sea. Some live in fresh water or on land.

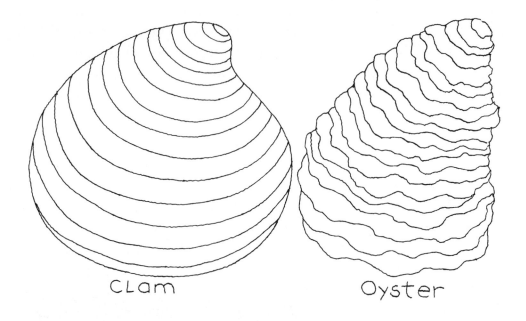

Clam   Oyster

Looking at Oysters and Clams

SHELL

Oysters and clams have a hard shell held together on top by a hinge. The oldest part of the shell is a thickened part near the hinge. It is called the *umbo*. The shell is the skeleton of these animals without backbones. They wear their skeleton on the outside. It protects them from the sea "weather," as well as from predators.

SHAPE

Oysters and clams are very well adapted to stay in one place. Clams burrow in mud or sand. Their flat shape makes burrowing easy. Oysters attach themselves to a hard surface.

GROWTH RINGS

The rings on the top shell of the oyster and clam look like the growth rings of a tree. Inside the shell, a thin tissue called the *mantle* covers the body and secretes the new shell material. The lines and bands produced in shell growth provide information about the age of the animal and the "weather" at the time of shell growth.

BODY

Oysters and clams have many of the same organs that we do—heart, stomach, intestines, sex organs, and kidneys. You will not be able to see the fleshy body, because it is inside the shell.

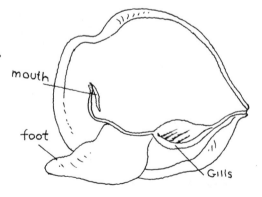

F O O T

The clam does not have toes, but its muscular foot works like a steam shovel —digging a hole for hiding in the soft bottom. The muscular foot acts like an anchor when its tip expands. Oysters don't have a foot.

M U S C L E S

For their size, clams and oysters have some of the strongest muscles in the world. The adductor muscles open and close the shell. The expressions "tight as a clam" and "clamming up" owe their origin to the strong adductor muscles. If you find a clam shell on the beach, you will see the round scars on the inside of the shell where the muscles were attached.

Eating and Breathing

Clams and oysters are filter feeders. They filter water through their gills for oxygen, and tiny plants called *phytoplankton* are passed on to the digestive system. An oyster pumps 300 gallons of water through its body daily.

The Pearl Factory

The human body tries to wall off any foreign object (like a splinter) that may enter it. In mollusks, a pearl forms when a foreign object— such as a grain of sand or a parasite—gets stuck between the shell and the mantle. The mantle covers the irritating particle with shell layers. Voilà! A pearl! Today more than 500 million pearls are cultivated artificially. A small piece of shell is placed in the oyster to start the process of pearl making.

Veterinarians'
BEHIND-THE-SCENES INFO

- In an aquarium, oysters are given gallons of water to filter daily to supply enough of their microscopic food.

- Oysters wall off any irritant that may get into the shell. The walling off process produces a pearl.

CLAM AND OYSTER STATS

Heaviest: Giant clam, 600 pounds

Biggest Pearl: 1½ inches

Making a Pearl: 3–5 years

HORSESHOE · CRABS

The horseshoe crab is not a true crab. In fact, it is more closely related to the spider and scorpion than to other kinds of crabs. Some people try to kill horseshoe crabs because they are afraid of them. Horseshoe crabs are harmless and should be respected for surviving unchanged for over 400 million years—they were here long before the dinosaurs!

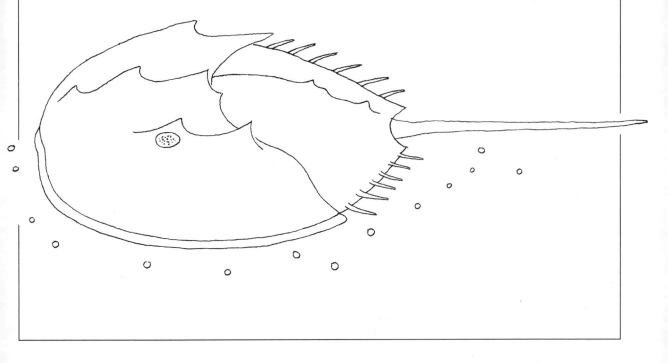

Looking at Horseshoe Crabs

S H E L L

The shell is shaped like a horseshoe. The color of the shell helps the horseshoe crab blend into the sandy bottoms where it lives. The shell is tough and jointed. This makes the horseshoe crab flexible, like a knight in a suit of armor.

E Y E S

Can you find the horseshoe crab's 9 eyes? The large eyes on each side of the shell are used to see in all directions. The small pair on the front of the shell and five others along its margin are light receptors but do not allow the horseshoe crab to see images.

G I L L S

Book gills, so named because they overlap like the pages of a book, are found behind the mouth and legs. These flattened, white structures remove oxygen from the water and excrete waste products like ammonia.

T A I L

The horseshoe crab's tail, or *telson*, is harmless and does not contain venom. It is used as a lever for the crab to right itself if it is flipped on its back, and also as an aid in swimming.

L E G S

The horseshoe crab's legs do the chewing. The mouth is hidden under the body, right in the middle of the five pairs of legs. Sharp spines on the base of the legs serve as teeth. These spines grind up worms and mollusks—but the mouth parts will function only if the legs are moving. Mother horseshoe crab to her son, who is running fast: "Honey, chew your food more slowly, please."

T H E   B A C K S T R O K E   C H A M P I O N

The horseshoe crab swims upside down. Its book gills, tail, feet, and jointed shell contribute to its graceful backstroke.

No Crabcakes, Please

Horseshoe crabs like to eat clams and worms.

Dating and Mating

Horseshoe crabs mate in the late spring in the shallow waters of bays and estuaries. The male's sperm covers the female's 200–300 blue-green eggs, which are the size of BBs. Thousands of eggs are laid, but shore birds make a quick meal of many of them. Two weeks after the eggs are fertilized, tiny larvae hatch. Those that survive and are not eaten settle to the bottom, eat, and grow.

Veterinarians' BEHIND-THE-SCENES INFO

- Horseshoe crabs are very hardy and have few medical problems.

- A sick horseshoe crab's gills will be "flappy"—they look as if they are working overtime.

HORSESHOE CRAB STATS

Life Span: 40 years

Egg Production: 50,000 per year

Hibernation: One-half year in the North

L·O·B·S·T·E·R·S

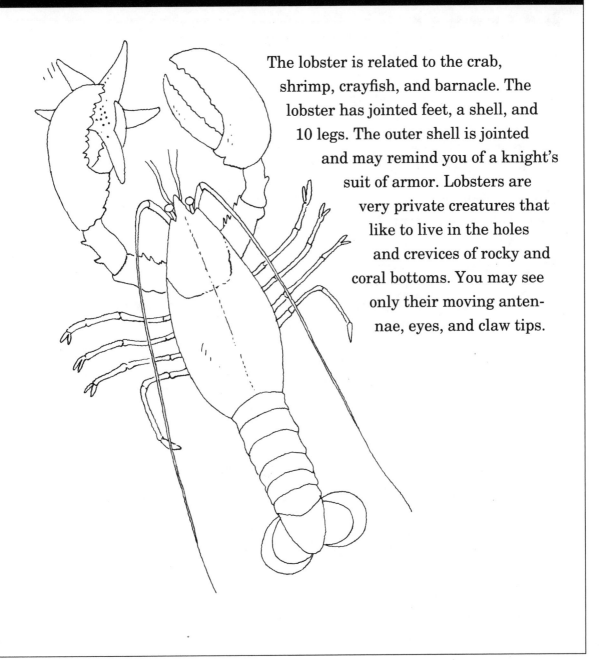

The lobster is related to the crab, shrimp, crayfish, and barnacle. The lobster has jointed feet, a shell, and 10 legs. The outer shell is jointed and may remind you of a knight's suit of armor. Lobsters are very private creatures that like to live in the holes and crevices of rocky and coral bottoms. You may see only their moving antennae, eyes, and claw tips.

Looking at Lobsters

ANTENNAE

The long antennae wave in the water, searching for chemical "scents" that may be an enemy, snack, or sexual partner. Fine hairs on the shell also help lobsters "smell" what is around them.

EYES

The lobster's eyes "pop out of its head." The two eyes are on movable stalks. Lobsters could use a pair of glasses. They can see images but not sharply. They can see movement. It is not known if lobsters can see in color.

MOUTH

The lobster's jaws are used for grinding and biting. You may see them moving on the bottom of the head.

CLAWS

Usually the lobster with the biggest claws is "top dog." The big front claws are used to crush and rip. Most lobsters are right-handed. The large crusher claw is on the right, and the small pincer is on the left.

SHELL

The shell is like a suit of armor. It contains the mineral calcium and is very hard. Green "color factories" called *chromatophores* give the lobster its greenish color. Live lobsters are brownish green. Cooked lobsters are red. Lobsters are boiled alive. This is not humane. People probably would not cook lobsters if lobsters could scream.

Moving Like a Lobster

- Lobsters walk forward, whereas crabs move sideways.

- Lobsters rarely swim.

- If caught in the open, the lobster can flex its powerful tail and spring back 3–5 feet in the water.

How Do You Know If a Lobster Is Getting "Crabby"?

- The lobster raises its claws.

- The lobster spreads its tail fins.

- The lobster stands tall on its legs.

Lobsters get aggressive during the mating season and when they feel threatened.

How a Lobster "Smells"

- Tiny antennae on the legs tell the lobster which way the current is going.

- The lobster lines up against the current, just as a land animal locates food and enemies by standing downwind to catch scents carried by the wind.

- The antennae sample the scents in the water. They smell the chemicals released by other sea life. Does this smell like clam chowder to a lobster?

Lobster Karate

- The lobster's large claw can break your finger.
- A snap from the tail can cut your hand.

Lobster Enemies

- Humans.
- Codfish.
- Toadfish.
- Sea robins.
- Skates.
- Seals.
- Other lobsters. Lobsters may be cannibalistic if they fight over territory or mates.

The Lobster Is a Messy Eater

- It tears and grinds its meal. Most is lost to currents and other fish.
- It likes "midnight snacks," eating only at night.

A Lobster's Dinner

- Clams, mussels, snails, marine worms, starfish, seaweed, and fish.
- Its all-time favorite meal is rock crabs.

Molting

- When lobsters outgrow their "clothes"—their outer shell—they molt.

- They wiggle out of their shells.

- The lobster feels like a soft sponge at this stage and is very vulnerable to being a "lobster dinner" for other sea creatures.

- The lobster immediately pumps its tissues full of water until it looks like a big water balloon. The claws are the last part to fill with water.

- The "lobster bluff": The lobster usually hides after it molts. If it moves, it walks around like "macho man," but he's a real softy. The outer shell takes a week to harden.

- Usually the lobster's first meal after hardening is its old shell. It has minerals that the lobster needs for growth.

- During its first year, the lobster molts about 9 times.

Mating, Lobster Style

- The female must be soft shelled (about 24 hours after a molt) to mate.

- The male must have molted earlier, and his shell must be harder than the female's.

- The female releases *pheromones* (sex attractant chemicals) into the water. This attracts and excites males.

- Because the female is newly molted and soft shelled, her partner must be careful.

The Courtship Dance

- The courtship ritual lasts half an hour.

- Head to head...turn around...head to head again. The male continuously strokes the female with his antennae.

- The male climbs up the female's back, turns her over with his walking legs, and extends his large claws straight out in front so they are out of the way.

- He deposits sperm in the female. This takes one minute.

"In Berry" and Beyond

- The female carries the sperm around for about one year and the fertilized eggs for another year.

- The female carries about 3,000 to 100,000 eggs. They look like a cluster of grapes. Carrying eggs is called being "in berry."

- Baby lobsters are the size of mosquitoes when they hatch.

- Fewer than 1 percent survive the first month. Most are eaten by predators.

- Baby lobsters stay out of sight for years, living in crevices and holes and feeding at night.

- It takes 7 years to become a 1-pound adult.

Veterinarians'
BEHIND-THE-SCENES INFO

- Red tail is an often fatal bacterial disease that can infect lobsters. Antibiotics are used in an attempt to treat it. The water is tested to see if there are any chemicals that could have caused the lobster's immune system to fail.

- Diet in captivity: Commercial pellet food and almost any raw seafood around.

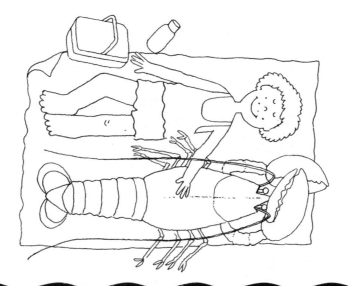

LOBSTER STATS

Length: Up to 5 feet

Weight: Up to 45 pounds

Life Span: Up to 100 years

Sexual Maturity: At 7 years

O·C·T·O·P·U·S·E·S

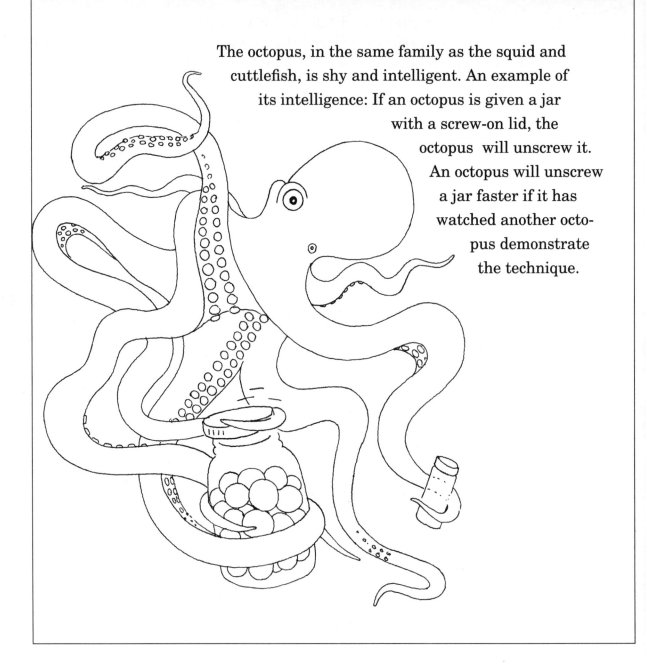

The octopus, in the same family as the squid and cuttlefish, is shy and intelligent. An example of its intelligence: If an octopus is given a jar with a screw-on lid, the octopus will unscrew it. An octopus will unscrew a jar faster if it has watched another octopus demonstrate the technique.

Looking at Octopuses

A R M S
....
The octopus has 8 arms—the better to hug you—for holding onto prey and other objects. The third right arm of the male transfers sperm to the female. Octopus arms will regrow if lost in a confrontation.

M O U T H
....
The octopus's parrotlike beak is found underneath its body, where all the arms meet.

B O D Y
....
The baglike body, behind the large eyes, houses all the internal organs.

The "Water Chameleon"

It's white...no...it's dark red...no, it's...The octopus can change into any of a rainbow of colors, depending on its mood or camouflage needs.

Can the Octopus Fit Through a Straw?

The octopus does not have a skeleton. So it is able to squeeze into small spaces.

Why Wouldn't the Octopus Be a Good Long-Distance Runner?

A struggling octopus runs out of oxygen quickly. The oxygen-carrying part of its blood is not very well developed.

Eeek...Ink !

To escape predators, the octopus squirts a black ink that acts like a smoke screen and takes on the shape of the octopus.

The Octopus Jet Ski

The octopus sucks water in and expels it through a siphon, becoming a "jet-propelled" octopus.

Octopus or Puss?

The octopus is considered as intelligent as a cat.

A Really Loving Parent

Mother octopus attaches her 80,000 eggs, in grapelike clusters, to the ceiling of her den. She flows oxygen-rich water over the eggs by shooting water through her siphon. She tenderly cleans the eggs with her arms. Each egg is the size of a grain of rice.

Having a "Taste" for Octopus

Whales, dolphins, seals, sea lions, sharks, moray eels, and other fish like to eat octopus.

A Tough Beginning and a Sad Ending

Only one or two of the 80,000 newborn octopuses live to become adults. The others are eaten by fish and other creatures. Mother octopus cares for her eggs for 6 months, until they hatch. She doesn't eat while she's guarding the eggs. Then she dies; she has lived her natural life span.

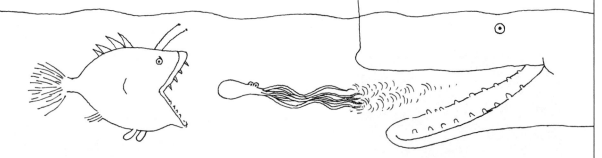

The Octopus Likes to Eat at Home

The octopus hunts crabs, abalone, salmon, or other fish at night. "You're stunning!" The octopus bites or drills into crabs, and injects a vemon that stuns them. It is not uncommon for an octopus to carry dozens of crabs in its webs, (the skin folds attached to the base of the arms) back to its den for a midnight snack.

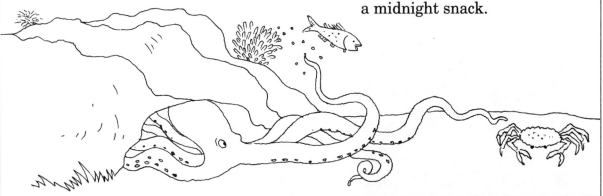

Octopuses

Veterinarians'
BEHIND-THE-SCENES INFO

- In the aquarium, the octopus is very happy to see its keepers and likes to play tug-of-war or just to hug the keeper's arm.

- The keepers love the octopuses and are sad when the female lays her eggs, because they know she will soon die.

- If antibiotic injections are needed, they are given in one of the arms.

- In the aquarium, the octopus is fed crabs and scallops.

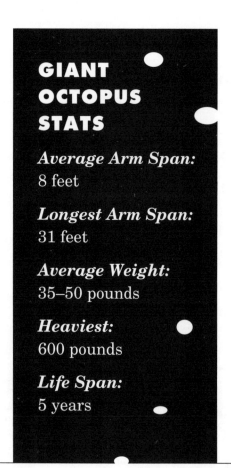

GIANT OCTOPUS STATS

Average Arm Span:
8 feet

Longest Arm Span:
31 feet

Average Weight:
35–50 pounds

Heaviest:
600 pounds

Life Span:
5 years

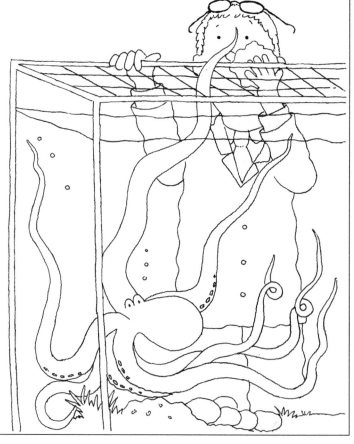

WATER · TURTLES

Water turtles spend most of their lives in or near water. They have been around for 200 million years, and are found around freshwater ponds, lakes, brackish water—a mixture of fresh water from the land and salt water from the ocean—and in the great oceans of the world.

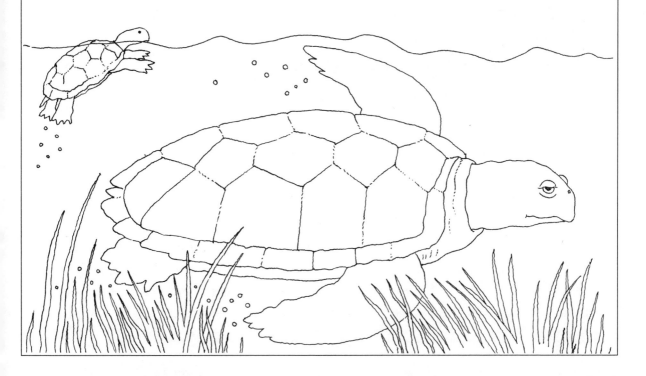

Looking at Water Turtles

S H E L L

Water turtles have flat shells—for less water resistance when swimming. The shell is a living structure, just like the turtle's bones or heart.

F E E T   A N D   L E G S

Sea turtles have strong, muscular, paddlelike flippers that cannot be pulled into the shell. Other water turtles have retractable legs, outfitted with toes, nails, and webbed feet.

S K I N

Sea turtles cannot retract their head and legs, so you will find that the skin is much thicker on the sea turtle than on other turtles—for extra protection.

M O U T H

Water turtles have no teeth, but they do have sharp, horny beaks to bite and crush frogs, crabs, snails, shrimp, fish, or other dinner delights.

Breathing Underwater

Turtles have lungs for breathing air. They can hold their breath for hours underwater, because their bodies use oxygen more slowly than those of humans. Some turtles can remove oxygen from water, because of special tissue in the back of the throat or in the anal area.

Salty Tears

Too much salt can be deadly—even for a sea turtle. Excess salt is excreted from tear glands.

New Life, Sea Turtle Style

- About 10–20 years after leaving it, sea turtles return to the beach where they were born, to lay their eggs.

- The 100 eggs, which look like Ping-Pong balls, are buried in a deep hole that the female digs.

- She returns to the sea, never seeing her offspring.

- On a cool night 2–3 months later, the young begin to hatch.

- They scramble up through the sand and dash to the sea with the help of the moon's reflection on the ocean.

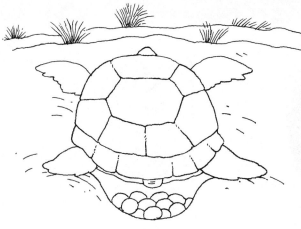

- Most turtles don't make it to adulthood. The odds are about 1 in 1,000.

- High tides, beach erosion, and plant erosion may destroy a nest. Predators such as crabs, sea birds, and large fish like to eat the eggs or the young turtles. Humans are the turtle's biggest threat.

Veterinarians'
BEHIND-THE-SCENES INFO

- Shell fractures can be repaired with dental acrylic or fiberglass.

- A turtle is radiographed (x-rayed) by taping it to an x-ray plate with the head and legs extended. If a turtle is having a problem with an internal organ or has swallowed a foreign object, a radiograph may be helpful.

WATER TURTLE STATS

Longest:
Leatherback turtle,
7 feet

Heaviest:
Leatherback turtle,
1,900 pounds

Smallest Sea Turtle:
Kemp's ridley,
95 pounds

Swimming Speed:
Sea turtles,
15 miles per hour

Life Span:
30–150 years

FROGS · TOADS · AND · SALAMANDERS

Frogs seem to be always smiling. Their hopping ability amazes us. Their "ribbit" love calls remind us of warm, cozy summer nights.

Frogs, toads, and salamanders are called *amphibians*, which means "double-life"— they are able to live on land and water at different times.

Amphibians were on the earth long before the dinosaurs, but the amphibian population, including frogs, is disappearing in many parts of the world. Acid rain, other pollutants, and habitat destruction may be responsible.

Looking at Frogs, Toads, and Salamanders

SKIN

Frogs and salamanders have a smooth, slippery skin, whereas toads have bumpy skin. The skin is more than a protective wrapping. Amphibians drink and breathe through their skin. They absorb oxygen from water or air. Toads resting under moist soil can even absorb the oxygen between soil particles.

LEGS

Frogs have long, muscular legs for jumping and swimming. Toads are not very athletic. Salamanders have quick little legs.

TOES AND FEET

There are no claws, but the tips are tough and strong—just right to hold onto slippery rocks or uncooperative meals. Webbed feet like flippers on the feet help frogs swim fast.

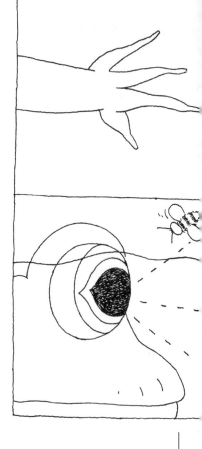

EARS

Frogs and toads do not have earlobes. Their eardrums are on the surface of the head, a large circle behind each eye. Male frogs usually have eardrums larger than their eyes. Salamanders don't even have eardrums, but they do have middle ear bones, like frogs and toads.

TONGUE

The frog's tongue is long and sticky, and it is attached at the front of the mouth. It is whipped out quickly to catch insects and other snacks.

TEETH

Yes...frogs have teeth on the top jaw, to hold onto their live meal.

EYES

Frog, toad, and salamander eyes are large, and these animals can see almost in a complete circle. The eyes are located high on the head, which helps frogs "keep an eye" on the situation—body under the water but watching for an insect delight. A clear membrane acts like swim goggles to protect the eyes underwater.

"Rib-bit, Rib-bit"...No Ribs

Frogs, toads, and salamanders don't have ribs. That's why their bellies feel so soft.

A Deadly Meal

Toads have large glands shaped like jelly beans behind each eye which secrete a bitter poison that may burn an animal's mouth. Some toads, such as *Bufo marinus*, have a poison that can kill a dog by stopping the heart.

Croaking for Love

All that croaking is the *male* frog's way of saying "I love you." Females never croak.

The Amphibian's Worst Nightmares

Snakes, rats, raccoons, birds (including herons and gulls), turtles, and fish eat frogs, toads, and salamanders.

The "Birds and the Bees"...and the Amphibians

- Hundreds or even thousands of eggs are laid in a jellylike clump in shallow water.

- The male fertilizes the eggs.

- The eggs hatch into tadpoles and polliwogs. They have gills, breathe like fish, and have a tail.

- Then they grow legs and lose their gills.

- Frogs and toads lose their tails. Salamanders keep their long tails.

Veterinarians'
BEHIND-THE-SCENES INFO

- Amphibians need a pool or a dish of water at all times so they do not get dehydrated.

- Amphibians need a cool area to retreat to if their environment gets too hot.

- If an amphibian needs to be anesthetized for surgery, it is immersed in an anesthetic solution.

- Frogs can be soaked in an antibiotic solution if they get a skin infection.

AMPHIBIAN STATS

Largest: Chinese giant salamander, 6 feet long

Heaviest: Chinese giant salamander, 143 pounds

Largest Toad: *Bufo marinus.* One, named Totally Awesome, was 10 inches, 5 pounds

Largest Frog: Goliath frog, 13 inches, 7 pounds

Smallest: Short-headed toad of Brazil, less than ½ inch

Most Poisonous: Golden dart-poison frog

Longest Frog Jump: Santjie, a South African sharp-nosed frog, jumped 33 feet 5½ inches*

Life Spans: Tiger salamander, 10 years; bullfrog, 6 years; American toad, 4 years

* *Guinness Book of World Records* (New York: Bantam, 1990)

Frogs, Toads, and Salamanders

W·A·T·E·R B·I·R·D·S

Many birds live on or near the water. Eating and raising the young are done by the sea, river, lake, or pond. Waterfowl, or water birds, include ducks, swans, geese, plovers, sandpipers, gulls, terns, pelicans, cormorants, herons, flamingos, loons, albatrosses, petrels, puffins, and penguins.

Looking at Water Birds

BEAK

The beak, or bill, is shaped perfectly for food gathering. It is the bird's spoon or fork. The duck's and swan's beaks are flat, to help scoop up food from the mud or water. How about the pelican's beak? The pelican dives in the water and gets a mouthful of fish in an expandable pouch when returning to the surface. That's a real million-dollar bill! The slightly hooked bill of the penguin is perfectly shaped to grab its seafood meals—fish, squid, and small shrimplike animals called krill. The seagull's long beak with the curved tip is a perfect utensil for fish, insects, or garbage!

LEGS

Long-legged birds usually wade and wait. The heron is often called the "spear on stilts." It stalks its prey in shallow water, pauses, then quickly thrusts out its crooked neck, grabbing a fish in its beak. The wood stork stretches out one leg in freshwater ponds and stirs up the fish and frogs,

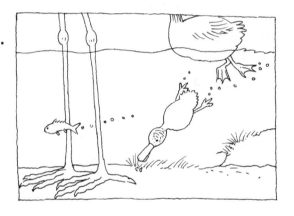

giving them a running start—a "meal on the run." Ducks, geese, and swans have short legs set back on the body—great for water cruising.

FEET

The long toes of herons and egrets help keep the birds from sinking in the muddy bottoms. Ducks, geese, gulls, puffins, and swans have webbed feet, which help them paddle on the surface, propel them underwater to feed, and help them get their footing on sand or other dry land areas.

Water off a Duck's Back

Water runs off a duck's back. Waterfowl are waterproof, due to oil that they spread on their feathers from an oil gland, and microscopic hooks that zip up each tight-fitting feather. Smooth layers of feathers cover the bird. A thick layer of small feathers, called down, protects water birds from the cold.

Feather Count

A whistling swan was found to have 25,216 feathers, of which 20,177 were on the head and neck (*Guinness Book of World Records, 1990*)

Floating Like a Balloon

Air sacs in the waterfowl's body help keep it floating. When the bird dives, the air is pumped out.

Preening

Birds are frequently busy straightening out and reconnecting their feathers. This is called preening. They also rub their beaks on an oil gland near the tail and comb the oil through each feather.

Camouflage

In nature, not being seen may mean not being eaten. Many animals have wonderful ways of blending in with their surroundings. Puffins and penguins wear black on their back and white on their undersides. This makes it difficult for their enemies to see them on the open ocean.

The bright light or the ice match the white belly feathers. The dark ocean blends in with the black back. The penguin's tuxedo protects it from predators (killer whales, sea lions, and fur seals).

Male or Female?

In general, in the bird world the males, when they are adults, are larger and more colorful than the females.

Veterinarians'
BEHIND-THE-SCENES INFO

- Herons have sharp, pointed beaks, which can cause eye damage to the handler if the head of the bird is not held firmly.

- Water birds are fed game-bird chow and greens. Pelicans eat mackerel, herring, and smelt.

- Crickets and mealworms are snack food.

- If water birds need to be examined, a hand net is used to restrain them so they will not injure themselves or others.

WATER BIRD STATS

Body Temperature: 106° F

Heart Rate: 200 beats per minute

Egg Sitting: About 25–30 days

Become Fully Feathered: In 2–3 months

(except swans—4 months)

Life Span: 20–30 years

Penguins

People love penguins. They act so human (or do we act so penguin?), all dressed up in their tuxedos. Penguins are flightless birds that look funny when they waddle on land, but are champion swimmers and divers. All penguins live in the Southern Hemisphere. Although most penguins (emperor and Adélie) live around the Antarctic Circle, some species are found on the coasts of South America, South Africa, New Zealand, and southern Australia. Some penguins, with less fatty blubber, are found in a much warmer climate—the Galápagos Islands on the equator.

A penguin now extinct weighed 300 pounds and was 5½ feet tall.

Peruvian Penguin

Looking at Penguins

WINGS
....

Penguins have small wings that are covered with tiny, tightly packed, oil-coated feathers. The wings are excellent waterproofed paddles for fast diving and swimming.

BODY SHAPE
....

A penguin is shaped like a submarine—perfect for fast swimming.

BONES
....

Birds that fly have hollow bones for lightness. Penguins don't fly and don't need to float very well. Their bones are solid, like human bones, helping them dive and swim fast.

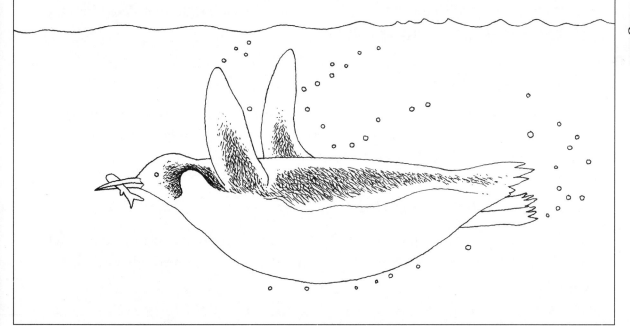

The Salt Gland

Penguins, like other sea birds, have a gland above their eyes that secretes the salt taken from the water that they drink and the food that they eat. The salt flows out, in a liquid form, down grooves in the beak and off the tip. If the excess salt was not eliminated from their bodies, the penguins would die.

Keeping Warm, the Penguin Way

Penguins keep warm by producing heat inside the body (they are warm-blooded animals). The feathers (70 per square inch) produce an insulating layer. A thick fat layer, called blubber, under the skin also keeps the birds warm.

Penguin Land Maneuvers

Penguins walk, run, or toboggan on land. Penguins waddle-walk very slowly—about 1½ miles per hour. When a penguin falls on its stomach and sleds across the snow, pushing with its wings and feet, it is called tobogganing. Penguins can toboggan as fast as a human can sprint.

Catching a Penguin

You have a better chance of catching a penguin on land than you do in water. Penguins zip through the water at 15 miles per hour. The fastest human would be far behind, at 5 miles per hour.

Acting Like a Porpoise

As they swim, penguins pop out of the water, take a breath, and plunge back in. The "porpoise" of this maneuver is to get the air they need without slowing down.

Dining Like a Penguin

In nature, some penguins may dive down more than 900 feet to catch large squid. Penguins are very good sea hunters; they feed on fish, squid, and krill. In aquariums, they are fed fish, mackerel, herring, smelt, and squid. A fish containing a vitamin-mineral supplement is fed first to each penguin to ensure that each penguin gets its daily vitamins.

Veterinarians'
BEHIND-THE-SCENES INFO

- Holding a penguin: It takes two people to hold a large penguin. The powerful wings can bruise you, and the strong, sharp bill can peck you full of holes.

- If a penguin needs medicine, the medicine is put in a single fish and fed to the patient.

- Refrigeration and ice blocks keep penguins' water cool during warm weather.

PENGUIN STATS

Height: Tallest—emperor, 3½ feet; smallest—little blue, 15 inches

Weight: Heaviest—emperor, 90 pounds; lightest—little blue, 2½ pounds

Sexual Maturity: At 2–4 years

Eggs Laid: 1–2

Incubation of Eggs: Humboldt, 35 days; emperor, 60 days

Life Span: 30 years

Seagulls

Gulls are very social birds. They don't mind sharing their feeding area with other birds, although they will screech, flap their wings, and jealously guard their food. They like to rest together and will signal—with a loud call to other birds—that they have found food.

Gulls give many of us a very happy feeling with their calls. The laughing gull sounds like he has a good joke that he wants to share with the world. Their ease of soaring in the wind reminds us of a freedom that we may wish that we had.

Free-flying gulls are not displayed in aquariums. Only gulls that have been injured and cannot fly would even be considered for display, since these birds would not survive in nature.

Looking at Gulls

FEATHERS

The tight feathering on the body is a great insulator and a waterproof "jacket." The wide, long, and pointed feathers at the wing tips are perfect for flapping, soaring, gliding, and skimming the water surface.

Being "Gull"-able

- Wings drooping and away from the body: "I'm angry!"

- Standing still and tall, and staring: "You're in my territory."

- Trumpet call with head lowered and neck extended, then head thrown back: "I dare you to come into my territory!"

Red Marks the Spot

When a gull chick pecks at a red spot near the parent's bill tip, it gets fed. Mother or father regurgitates food for the chick.

The Gull Restaurant

Gulls are scavengers. They'll eat seafood, insects, and...garbage. Do you think that they would like a peanut butter and jellyfish sandwich?

Veterinarians'
BEHIND-THE-SCENES INFO

- In nature, gulls and other water birds may eat objects that come from human pollution—golf tees, glass, old inner-tube scraps, fishing line, or hooks. Surgery or endoscopy (using a flexible telescope-like instrument) must be done to remove the object and save the bird.

- Oil spills kill birds. The oil pastes their feathers, eyes, and nostrils, stresses them, is toxic, and blocks their intestines. This results in drowning or starvation.

- Oil-covered birds are treated for shock, dehydration, and starvation with fluids containing sugar (dextrose) or ground fish. The oil is removed with such products as Amber Lux. Then the bird is rinsed. The process is repeated until the bird is clean.

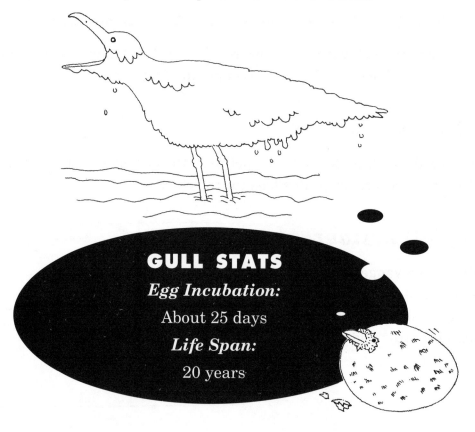

GULL STATS

Egg Incubation:

About 25 days

Life Span:

20 years

Puffins

Puffins spend most of their lives on the sea in the far North, but in the summer they come ashore to reproduce. Large colonies of puffins can be found on remote islands off the coasts of Alaska and Washinton, northern Maine, Canada, Iceland, Newfoundland, and northern Europe. They are called "sea parrots," because their parrotlike beaks blossom with a rainbow of colors during the breeding season.

LOOKING AT PUFFINS

B E A K

During the breeding season, puffins' beaks and plumage become very colorful—to attract the opposite sex.

N O S T R I L S

Puffins drink salt water. Their nasal salt glands excrete the extra salt.

P U F F I N   P A S T I M E S

Puffins like to dive, swim, preen, bathe, sleep, eat, and drink.

Parlez-Vous Puffin?

Puffins "speak" with their bodies:

❶ Beak tapping—"kissing"

❷ Beak gaping—the puffin threat

❸ The strut—feeling brave

❹ Head jerk—excitement

❺ The low crouch—fear

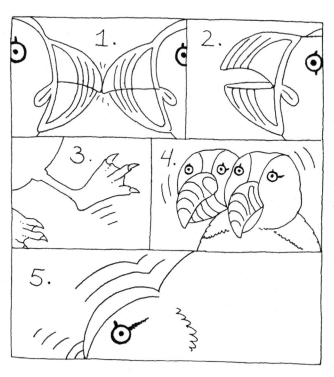

Drinking Like a Chicken

A puffin sips water like a barnyard rooster, tipping its head back to let the water flow down the throat.

One Good "Tern" Deserves Another

Terns are aggressive little birds. They help protect puffin eggs and their chicks from being eaten by seagulls by "dive bombing" the gulls.

Bye-bye, Mom and Dad

Puffin parents produce only one chick yearly. They drop off fish at the burrow or rocky crevice nest entrance for their one chick. The chick leaves the nest at 40 days and swims away in the middle of the night, never to see its parents again.

Home Is Where the Heart Is

The puffin returns to its birthplace when it is 5 years old, to start its own family.

Veterinarians'
BEHIND-THE-SCENES INFO

- Puffin exhibits have to be kept c-c-cold! The temperature is around 42° F.

- Mirrors are used to encourage breeding. Puffins like company—a large colony is best. The mirror produces "instant puffins."

- The puffins are hand fed twice daily.

- They are fed herring, capelin, smelt, and krill.

- Puffins can be kept in fresh water. If they are, the glands that would usually filter salt out of the water shrink.

PUFFIN STATS

Diving Ability:
To a depth of about 250 feet

Underwater Time:
About 2 minutes

Weight:
1 pound

Sexual Maturity:
At 5 years

Life Span:
20 years

MARINE · MAMMALS

Cetaceans (whales, dolphins, and porpoises), pinnipeds (seals, sea lions, and walruses), sea otters, and manatees are marine mammals. They are warm-blooded animals that breathe air, have hair, and nurse their young. Each group is thought to have evolved from a different land animal that moved back to the sea. The cetaceans probably descended from a cowlike animal. The pinnipeds are descended from otterlike ancestors of the weasel family, and the sea otter is related to land otters. The manatee has elephantlike ancestors. Definitive facts about these animals' origins will probably be found someday through DNA analyses.

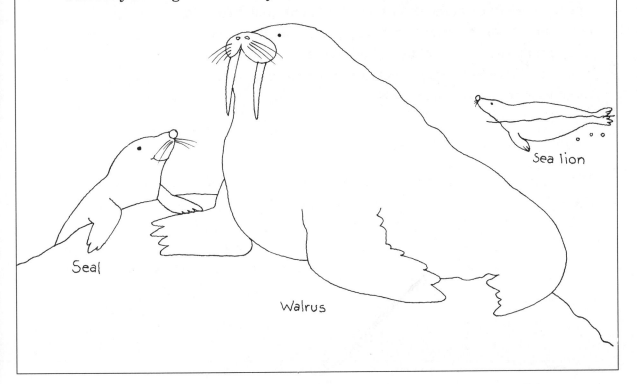

Seal

Walrus

Sea lion

Looking at Marine Mammals

B R E A T H I N G

Marine mammals do not have gills. They have breathing tubes and lungs, just like most land animals.

H A I R

All marine mammals have hair somewhere. Whales, porpoises, and dolphins have hair (whiskers on the snout) only when they are infants. Manatees have sparse hair on the head and upper lip.

Warm-Blooded Animals

Marine mammals make their own body heat, just like land mammals. Some seals, all cetaceans, and manatees get help from a thick layer of fat called blubber. There is much that is not known yet about temperature regulation in marine mammals.

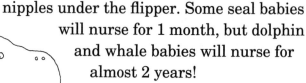

Nursing Their Babies

Marine mammals are born like human babies, not from eggs. They get milk from their mothers. The manatee, for example, nurses its baby with milk from nipples under the flipper. Some seal babies will nurse for 1 month, but dolphin and whale babies will nurse for almost 2 years!

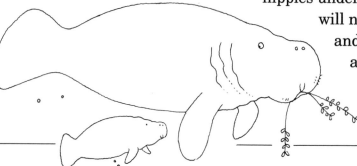

Sea Otters

The sea otter's home ranges from the Kuril Islands to Prince William Sound off Alaska. There are small colonies of sea otters off the coasts of Washington State and Vancouver Island. A colony of 1,500 lives off the coast of central California. There were once 20,000 off the coast until commercial fur hunters brought the sea otter to the brink of extinction during the 1700s and 1800s. Today there are only about 150,000 sea otters in the world. There were probably millions in the 1700s. Modern threats to the survival of the sea otter are oil spills, gill nets, and human activity in and near the sea. The sea otter depends on our sensitivity and protection for its survival.

Looking at Sea Otters

F U R

The *thick*, brown fur is made up of two layers. It is so thick that it can have 1,000,000 hairs in 1 square inch, more than on any other animal on the earth. A dog has about 30,000–60,000 hairs per square inch. The coat helps the otter keep a toasty 100° F body temperature in icy water (35° F to 60° F). The sea otter does not have a thick fat or blubber layer for insulation. Air bubbles trapped in the hair coat help keep the otter buoyant, dry, and warm.

F E E T

The hind feet are flipperlike—large and webbed. They make wonderful paddles. The front feet are small but very important for food gathering and grooming.

E Y E S

The otter's eyes look like little beads, ut they are super eyeballs. The eye has a special outer covering for protection and a lens that adjusts so that the otter can see underwater. A special lining that reflects light is found in the back of the eye (as in cats and dogs) so that seeing is possible in dark or murky water.

WHISKERS

The long whiskers are sensitive to vibrations in the water and help the otters feel in the dark.

Otter Space

Otters like to float together in groups, called rafts. There may be 20 or up to 2,000 otters in a raft.

Otter Beds—Kelp Help

Sea otters like to sleep in kelp beds, wrapping themselves in kelp "blankets" for coziness and so they will not drift. Drifting off to sleep is okay, but drifting while asleep could be dangerous. The otters could be eaten by a shark or a killer whale.

The Otter Menu

Sea urchins, crabs, mollusks (especially abalones), and some fish are the otter's favorite foods. A stone is frequently used as an "anvil" on its chest to break open shellfish. An 80-pound sea otter eats 25 pounds of food daily. That is the equivalent of a 200-pound man eating over 60 pounds of food a day!

The "Head Jerk"

The adult sea otter says hello, and checks the social status or sex of other sea otters, by burying its nose in the recipient's chest and belly and rapidly jerking its head from side to side. Do you think that the otter would find our greetings—handshakes, hugs, and kisses—silly?

The Belly Flop

Otters spend most of their time floating on their backs. When they are in a hurry, they swim belly down.

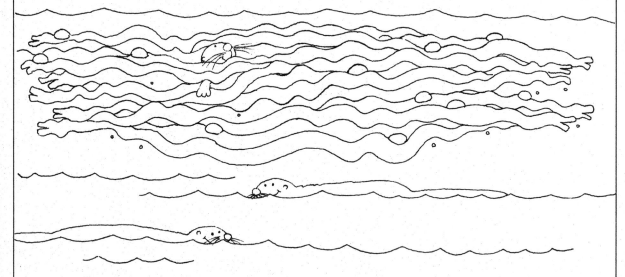

Otter Love

- Otters mate in the summer and fall.

- The female usually gives birth to one pup.

- Otter mothers are very caring.

- The male does not take part in caring for the pup.

- The pup has learned to dive and take care of itself by 6 months of age.

Veterinarians'
BEHIND-THE-SCENES INFO

- Otters are curious and playful. Everything must be attached in their exhibit; otherwise, starfish are used as Frisbees and sea anemones become small, round footballs. A basketball makes a perfect toy.

- Baby otters in the aquarium live on waterbeds to simulate the ocean environment.

- Baby otters follow their mother's example in learning feeding, grooming, and other survival skills. In a sea otter rescue program, pups learn these skills from a human "surrogate otter mother" in snorkeling gear.

- The aquarium menu is black cod, whitefish, squid, shrimp, crab, and geoduck clams. Yummy!

SEA OTTER STATS

Weight: *55 pounds*

Length: *4 feet*

Body Temperature: *100° F*

Underwater Time: *5 minutes*

Deepest Dive: *Over 300 feet*

Sexual Maturity: *At 3–5 years*

Gestation (Pregnancy): *4–6 months*

Life Span: *10–20 years*

Pinnipeds:
SEALS, SEA LIONS, AND WALRUSES

Sea lions and other "eared seals," "earless" seals (which do not have ear flaps), and walruses are called *pinnipeds*, or "fin-footed" marine mammals. Sea lions live all over the world. There are about 50,000 California sea lions in existence. They are found on rocky or sandy beaches from Vancouver Island, British Columbia, to the Tres Marías Islands off the coast of Mexico. The common harbor seal is an earless seal. It lives on the coasts of Europe, Canada, and the United States. The walrus, bigger than any other pinniped except the elephant seal, lives in the north Pacific and Atlantic regions. There are about 15,000 Pacific walruses in the Alaskan waters.

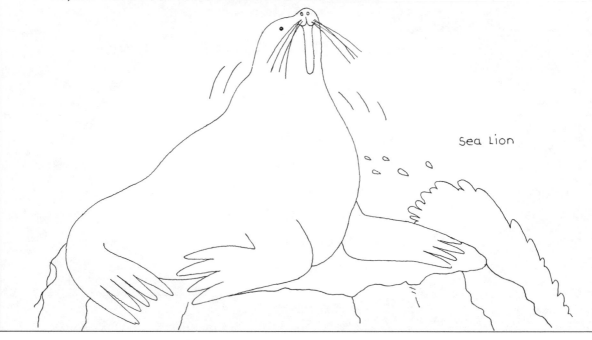

Sea Lion

Looking at Pinnipeds

FLIPPERS

The true, or "earless," seal moves like a caterpillar—humping along—on land. The back flippers are useless on land. All the flippers are small. In the water the true seal is very fast. The eared pinnipeds (sea lions and fur seals) have big, powerful front and back flippers. On land, the back flippers are rotated forward and used for walking.

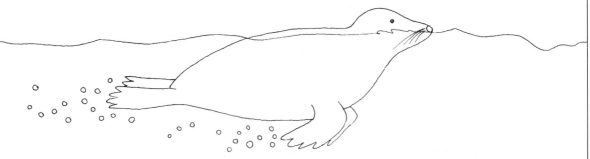

EARS

The true seals, such as the common harbor seal, do not have ear flaps. The sea lions, fur seals, and walruses have ear flaps.

BLUBBER

There is a 1- to 5-inch fat layer, called blubber, under the skin. This "fat coat" keeps pinnipeds warm.

TEETH

The long canine teeth have rings inside them that can be used to tell how many birthday candles should be on the cake.

Hot Days Are Worse Than Cold Days

Pinnipeds must be kept cool. They are prone to heat stroke. During hot days, seals may spread the webs of their hind flippers or wave or fan the flippers to keep cool. Shade, as well as cool water for bathing and drinking, must be provided.

Diving Champions

We still don't understand exactly what happens to a seal when it makes deep dives. The seal's heart rate drops to 10 beats per minute. Stored oxygen is directed to the heart, lungs, and brain so the seal doesn't need to breathe. Even though these adaptations are possible, most seal dives are short. In contrast, large sperm whales may stay underwater for up to 2 hours without taking a breath.

The Eligible Bachelor

In the wild, a male pinniped collects a harem of 10–20 females after staking out a territory on the beach. He patrols the borders of his territory to keep out other males. He may not leave it to feed for 3 months.

Pinniped Pools

The best pinniped pools in aquariums are filtered with sand and gravel filters. Some are kept clean by circulating and replacing the water. Others are kept clean by draining and replacing the water. Chemicals are added to keep a low bacteria level, just as we do with swimming pools. The water is tested for bad chemicals and bacteria every day.

Bearable Facts

The "eared seals" and walruses come from a line of ancestors related to bears. The common harbor seals are probably related to the sea otter.

"Seal" of Approval

In nature, seals eat fish. Polar bears eat seals.

Veterinarians'
BEHIND-THE-SCENES INFO

- Telemetry pills can be used to determine a pinniped's body temperature. After a pill has been swallowed, it sends out a radio signal from inside the body.

- Orphaned baby seals can be reared on a diet of whipped cream and blended whole herring. Clams are added to a walrus pup's diet. The baby bottle is hidden behind a barrier so that the pup does not get attached to a human.

- Small seals can be restrained with nets. Sea lions and walruses must be restrained in squeeze cages (metal cages with movable sides).

- Pinnipeds can be transported by airplanes, in shipping crates. They must be kept cool and wet, and provided with drinking water.

- Pinnipeds are very good at hiding illness. In the wild, it is important not to advertise weakness, so as not to be eaten. In the aquarium setting, the animal keeper and veterinarian must look very carefully for signs of illness—for example, neck stretching and coughing; back arching; changes in feeding, walking, or swimming behavior; changes in bowel movements or urine.

- Squid is a good laxative for pinnipeds.

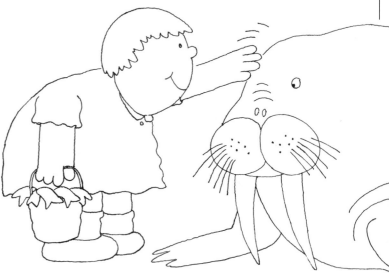

PINNIPED STATS

Body Temperature:	*98° F*
Heart Rate:	*60–80 beats per minute*
Breathing Rate:	*6–14 breaths per minute*
Weight:	*California sea lion, 170 pounds (female) to 450 pounds (male); common harbor seal, 275 pounds; walrus, 1,700 pounds (female) to 2,800 pounds (male)*
Sexual Maturity:	*Male at 5 years; female at 4 years*
Gestation (Pregnancy):	*Sea lion, 342–85 days; harbor seal, 270–330 days; walrus, 342 days*
Life Span:	*Sea lion, 13–25 years; harbor seal, 10–15 years; walrus, 30 years*

Cetaceans:
WHALES, PORPOISES, AND DOLPHINS

Whales, porpoises, and dophins are called *cetaceans*. Our fascination with dolphins is as old as our contact with the sea. The ancient Greeks had a story of a young boy being saved from drowning in the sea by a dolphin. Dolphins have been known to keep shipwrecked people company. One remarkable dolphin was reported to have followed ships back and forth across the Atlantic for 30 years.

Whales and other marine mammals have been on the earth for 20 million years. For 20 million years, cetaceans have lived in harmony with nature. In only 100 years, humans have threatened the survival of many species of whales and dolphins.

Looking at Whales, Porpoises, and Dolphins

BODY SHAPE

The body shape is considered perfect for traveling through water. It is smooth, streamlined, and tapered.

SKIN

The skin is smooth and feels like rubber. There are no hairs on the skin, although a newborn calf has a few bristles on its snout. These whiskers may be a remnant from its ancient land-based past.

FRONT FLIPPERS

The front legs are paddlelike flippers, which are used for steering, balancing, and stopping, but not for power to move through the water. There are five bony "fingers" inside the flippers.

TAIL

Power to move through the water is provided by the upstroke of the tail, or flukes.

M O U T H

Dolphins, porpoises, and orcas and beluga whales are called toothed whales since they have closely spaced teeth. The teeth develop during the first few months of life, and gradually wear with age. The teeth have rings like those of a tree and are useful for determining age. Baleen whales have no teeth, but have a strainer that looks like a large brush. They eat microscopic sea plants and animals called plankton. The blue whale is a baleen whale.

B O D Y   C O L O R

The toothed whales are usually dark on top and light-colored on the bottom. If viewed from below, the toothed whale blends in with the sun above. If viewed from above, the toothed whale blends in with the dark water below; this makes it easier for the whale to sneak up on a snack.

T H E   B L O W H O L E

The blowhole is like a nose on top of the head. The nasal passage leads to air sacs, a larynx (voice box), a trachea (windpipe), and a pair of lungs—much as in humans.

Dolphin or Porpoise?

The dolphin has a stubby snout, and the porpoise has a long flat snout.

Sound Advice

Some cetaceans use sound waves to move in dark oceans, find food, and communicate with one another. Clicking sounds, thought to originate in air spaces in the head, pass through an oil-filled area in the forehead and then out into the water. The sound waves bounce off an object and return by way of the jawbone to the inner ear. This process is called *echolocation*. It seems that the whale can interpret the shape, material, and distance of objects very quickly. Sound travels very fast in water—about 1 mile per second.

Dolphin "Aunties"

When a dolphin mother is giving birth, the other females, called "aunties," give moral support and help her along. On land, elephant aunties protect and care for the baby elephants in their herd in the same way.

Veterinarians'
BEHIND-THE-SCENES INFO

- Glass thermometers are not used to take a whale's temperature. If the whale squirms, the thermometer could break. A long, flexible thermometer is used.

- Blood samples are taken from the tail fluke or "front legs" (flippers), if needed. Dolphins are trained to jump up on a platform and present their tail or flipper for a blood sample.

- The dolphin is trained to present its "nose" (blowhole) for examination. It can keep its blowhole open during the examination.

- A foul odor from the blowhole, an increased breathing rate, and a fever may indicate pneumonia. Large doses of antibiotics and fluids are given to treat the infection.

- Stethoscopes are used to listen to the lungs of small whales, such as dolphins. A stethoscope would not be helpful on an orca. It would not even reveal whether the animal was alive, much less sick, since you couldn't hear anything through the thick blubber layer.

- The age of a whale can be determined by counting the rings of a tooth split lengthwise. Each ring, like a tree ring, indicates a year of age.

- If a whale is stranded on a beach at low tide, portable pumps and a fire hose may be used to keep the whale from getting overheated or dehydrated until it can be otherwise helped.

- A stranded whale may be given 20–30 gallons of fish gruel three times a day. That's a big deli belly!

- A satellite tracking device can be placed on the dorsal fin of a stranded whale that is to be returned to the ocean, to track its movement and its survival.

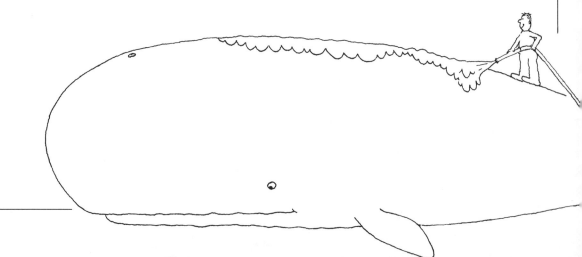

MARINE MAMMAL STATS

Speed: *Bottlenose dolphin, 20 miles per hour*
Common dolphin, 70 miles per hour

Length: *Bottlenose dolphin, 14 feet*
Orca, 32 feet
Sperm whale (not seen in aquariums), 70 feet
Blue whale (not seen in aquariums), 100 feet

Weight: *Bottlenose dolphin, 1,500 pounds*
Orca, 16,000 pounds
Humpback whale (not seen in aquariums), 105,000 pounds
Sperm whale, 120,000 pounds
Blue whale, 280,000 pounds

Body Temperature: *Bottlenose dolphin, 98.6° F (same as humans)*

Life Span: *Orca, 20 years, dolphin, 30 years*

Heart Rate: *Dolphin, 120–50 beats per minute*

Number of Teeth: *Bottlenose dolphin, 74–102, Killer whale, 40–56*

Sexual Maturity: *Bottlenose dolphin at 6 years*

Gestation (Pregnancy): *Bottlenose dolphin, 365 days*
Orca, 330–360 days

Nursing: *Whales and dolphins, 12–16 months*

Leaping Ability: *Dolphin, 16 feet*

Deep-Dive Breathing: *Dolphin, 1 breath every 15 minutes; sperm whale, 1 breath every 1½ hours. (It can dive down 2 miles!)*

C·O·R·A·L R·E·E·F·S

For color, beauty, shapes, forms, and variety of living things, few natural areas can equal coral reefs. Millions of creatures live in or on these underwater cities. Every inch of space is occupied by living things. Each creature in a coral reef is important to its survival.

The main builders are animals called coral *polyps*. They have soft bodies. Their tentacles capture drifting small plants and animals, called plankton.

Tiny algae called *zooxanthellae* grow inside the coral polyps. These plants use the sun to make food through a process called *photosynthesis*. This energy is then passed on to the coral polyps and helps them grow. They use minerals from seawater to build hard, white limestone protective homes around themselves.

In the aquarium, some of the coral reefs look real but are made of fiberglass; some are living coral. Using living coral has two drawbacks: living coral is difficult to maintain, and removing it from the ocean floors is destructive to our environment.

Looking at Coral Reefs

REEF CITY

The coral polyps form the basic reef
home with their hard outer limestone
tubes. Other groups—such as sponges,
algae (red, brown, and green),
anemones, clams, sea cucumbers, and
starfish—also contribute to the city-
like buildings.

CORAL REEF FISH

Fish in a rainbow of colors and patterns live among the coral reefs. They are
important to the reefs' health. Their grazing activity prevents the overgrowth
of algae. Some of the fish nibble on coral, and others are carnivores. Each
contributes to recycling and helps keep "reef city" in balance.

Keeping in Shape

Reef fish use their shapes to their advantage. Small, slender fish, such as
damsels and wrasses, hide in cracks to protect themselves from predators
and to surprise their small crustacean and worm snacks. Triggerfish use
their wedge-shaped heads to pick food from tight spots on the reef.

Reefs in the Arctic? No!

Although corals are found in all the oceans of the world, reefs are found
only in the tropics. The tiny algae called zooxanthellae that live in the coral
animals and are needed to build the reefs are found only in the warm,
light-filled tropical waters.

The Cleaning Station Business

Cleaning behavior, removing external parasites from fish, occurs on all reefs. The cleaner fish (or shrimp) set up "cleaning stations" on a prominent coral head or boulder. They advertise their presence through bright colors. The fish to be cleaned comes to the cleaning area, and the cleaner picks off parasites (even in the mouth or gills) while the fish remains motionless. Fish even line up, as if at a car wash, to wait their turn for cleaning. The parasites are the cleaner fish's food.

Parrots with Beaks

The beautiful parrot fish has a bony "beak" that it uses to crunch the coral. If you have a chance to watch it eat, you'll see it digest the algae which comes out the other end as sand.

The Fish Beauty Contest

The colors and patterns of the reef fish serve as camouflage and warning coloration, and for species recognition.

Night and Day on the Reef

During the day, parrot fish, groupers, and butterfly fish are among the active crowd. The nighttime belongs to moray eels, lobsters, sea urchins, octopuses, and coral polyps. The daytime inhabitants find cozy holes and crevices in the reef to rest and hide in.

Reef Relief

Reefs can exist and grow only if the following conditions are met:

- There must be water currents to prevent sediment and algae from covering the corals, increase oxygen and food delivery, and keep the water clear (for sunlight to penetrate). Sunlight is important for the zooxanthellae.

- The water temperature must be 76–78° F.

- The salt content of the water must be just right: 32–35 percent. There are exceptions, however; the salt content of the water is 42 percent in the Persian Gulf, yet it has coral reefs.

- The depth must be right. Since light is important, coral reefs do not develop in water that is deeper than 150 feet.

- Coral reefs can't be exposed to air for more than a few hours. Thus, they can't grow higher than the level of the lowest tides.

Veterinarians'
BEHIND-THE-SCENES INFO

Keeping corals alive in the aquarium requires re-creating the conditions that are found in nature. Here is how it is done at the National Aquarium in Baltimore.

- Light—special Gro-Lites are used, which produce the ultraviolet rays needed by the tiny zooxanthellae algae.

- Currents—a moving paddle pushes water back and forth over the coral reef.

- Water chemistry—water samples to check temperature, salt content, and quality are tested regularly.

- Keeping the water clean—the water is treated with ozone, filter systems are used, and algae are grown (for food) in a separate chamber called an algae scrubber.

- Feeding coral—newly hatched brine shrimp are automatically added to the water every 30 minutes by a small pump.

- Grazing algae—the growth of green algae is kept down by fish, sea urchins, and other grazers.

CORAL REEF STATS

Largest: *Great Barrier Reef, Australia, 1,200 miles long*

Oldest: *Eniwetok, Marshall Islands, 60 million years old*

Average Coral Reef Height: *100 feet*

K·E·L·P F·O·R·E·S·T·S

The kelp forests look like Amazon rain forests. The massive treelike plants are brown algae found in cold offshore waters. They grow upward from the bottom and spread their blades on the surface of the water so they can get a lot of light. These blades form a canopy similar to that in the Amazon rain forest—though you won't find any monkeys swinging in the kelp forest canopies. Giant kelp forests are found on the Pacific coast of both North and South America. Sea otters love them.

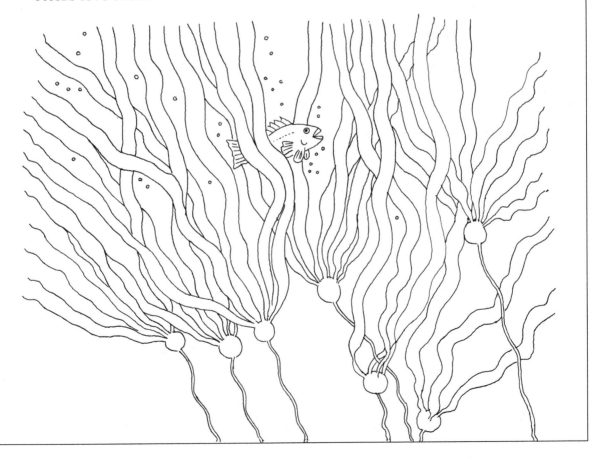

Looking at Kelp Forests

"F E E T"

Kelp anchor themselves to the bottom with a footlike structure called a *holdfast*. Unlike trees, they do not have a true root system.

S T E M S

The giant kelp have bodies like tree trunks. They have to be strong and flexible to withstand the strong ocean currents.

"B A L L O O N S"

The "leaves," called blades, float on the surface, because they contain gas-filled floats.

To Grow, the Kelp Forests Need:

- A hard surface for attachment.
- Light.
- Fairly clear water for light penetration.
- Cool water.

Feeding a Kelp Forest

Kelp make food through photosynthesis, and also get it directly from the seawater that constantly moves by them.

The "Fall" Season

Most kelp are perennial plants—they lose their blades and stems about once a year, and regrow new ones from the holdfast.

Threats to Kelp:

- Waves.
- Storms.
- Sea urchins.

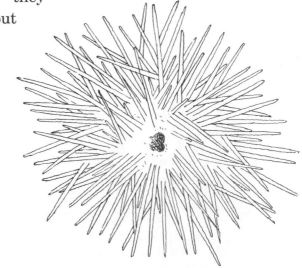

KELP FOREST STATS

Growth Rate: *20 inches per day*

Height: *60–90 feet*

Life Span: *7 years*

Water Trouble

- We are polluting the world's waters, threatening the survival of trees and other plants, insects, animals, and other living things.

- Factory wastes and sewage sludge (containing traces of pesticides, heavy metals, PCBs, organic chemicals, and human pathogens) are contaminating water life.

- Water in the ground (groundwater) is being polluted by pesticides used on our lawns and on farms, and by leaking landfills containing wastes from factories and homes.

- Gases from factory and automobile fuels mix with water to make acid rain. This rain pollutes rivers and lakes and kills fish. Animals that depend on these fish may starve.

- Oil spills and radioactive wastes pollute water, hurting or killing the birds, fish, and other living things that depend on that water.

- We have already helped some sea creatures fight to survive. Rivers and lakes have been cleaned so animals can live in them again. There are as many gray whales now as before whaling.

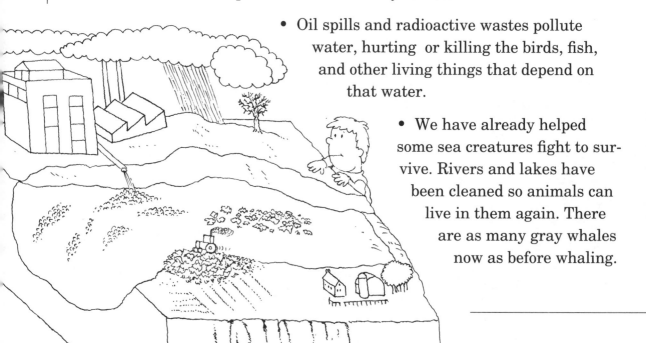

There are new puffin and sea otter colonies. Many people worked to make these things happen. Join them.

Saving the Turtle

- Stop hunting the turtle for its eggs, meat, leather, and shell for tortoiseshell jewelry, and for making face creams, soaps, and cosmetics.

- Preserve the beaches where turtles have returned for millions of years to lay their eggs.

- Preserve the rivers, streams, marsh-lands, and forests where turtles live.

- Use safer nets for commercial fishing, so turtles won't get caught and drown.

The Future of the Horseshoe Crab

- The horseshoe crab has been on earth for over 400 million years, but the loss of beach areas for egg laying threatens its survival.

Hope for the Sea Otter

- There are only about 1,800 California sea otters in the wild. Their larger cousins, the Alaskan sea otters, are doing better. There are 17,500 of them.

- Controlling the harvesting of shellfish (the sea otter's main food) by fishermen may save the sea otter.

- Oil spills are a major concern, so offshore drilling must be discouraged and safer oil tankers must be made.

The Puffin's Future

- The world's puffin population is decreasing.

- Puffins are hunted by humans for meat and feathers.

- Puffins are killed in oil spills and in fishermen's nets.

- Puffins' favorite foods, herring and capelin, are being overfished by fishermen—making it difficult for puffins to feed their chicks.

The Shark's Future

- Sharks have been on the earth for 400 million years, but the last 15 years have been very bad for them and many species may be on the road to extinction because of humans' misunderstanding and cruelty.

- Sharks are being overfished. Shark fin soup is an Asian delicacy. The dorsal (top) fin is cut off and the animal is thrown back into the ocean to die. Shark filets are becoming popular in the United States. Hunting sharks for sport is increasing.

- Sharks' gestation period (pregnancy) is about a year, and sharks produce few young.

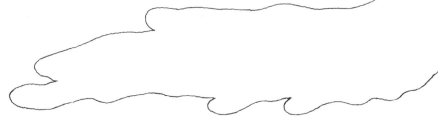

- You don't have to be a math whiz to see that fewer adults and fewer young = trouble for sharks.

- There are about 100 shark attacks a year, but there are about 4.5 million shark killings by humans yearly!

Saving the Cetaceans

- More than a million dolphins and porpoises die each year in fishnets that are used to catch fish or squid.

- Some of the fishnets are 40 miles long and are so large that they could circle Manhattan; 25,000 miles of nets are used in a year, enough to ring the earth.

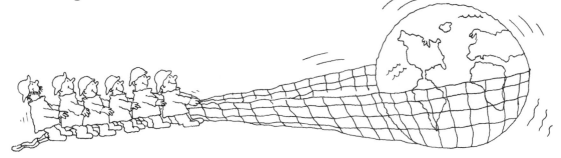

- Industrial chemicals and garbage dumped in the oceans may be affecting the dolphin population.

- The Indus River dolphin of Pakistan, the baiji (BAY-gee) of China, the black dolphin of Chile, and the Mexican porpoise are close to extinction because of river pollution and fishnets. The development and ongoing deforestation of the tropical rain forests endanger two dolphins, the boto and the tucuxi, which live in the Amazon and Orinoco rivers of Brazil.

- Whales have been hunted and killed for hundreds of years for oil and meat. Some whales, including the blue whale, are close to extinction. A few countries want to start whaling again. There is no good reason for killing whales. We have other sources for oils and meat.

Where Are the Frogs and Toads?

- The golden toad of Costa Rica was last seen in 1989.

- The amphibian population, including frogs, has dramatically decreased. Amphibians breathe through their skin. Acid rain, other pollutants, and habitat destruction may be responsible. The disappearance of frogs is bad news for all living things.

Where Are the Clams, Oysters, Lobsters, Crabs, and Fish?

- Overfishing and pollution are destroying the richness of our water world.

Help Save the Manatee

- Don't use motorboats in manatee areas.

- Protest filling, dredging, and dumping around manatee homes.

Saving the World's Coral Reefs

- Stop sewage pollution, open-ocean dumping, and offshore oil spills.

- Stop mining coral reefs for building material, as is done in countries such as India.

- Stop dynamiting to stun fish and capture them for the hobby trade and pet stores, as is done in some areas of the Philippines.

It takes a reef 50–100 years to recover from man-made damage or natural disasters such as hurricanes, typhoons, or a population explosion of sea stars, which eat coral.

Conserve Water

- The United States uses 400 billion gallons of water each day.

- We use 50–70 gallons each time we shower.

- Brushing your teeth, with the water running—2 gallons.

- A leaking faucet—more than 50 gallons per day.

- Washing your car with a hose— 150 gallons of water. If you use a sponge and bucket, you will use only 15 gallons.

Saving Our Wetlands

- The world's wetlands are being rapidly destroyed for farming, home building, and mining.

- Wetlands are areas that are frequently covered by water. Swamps, marshes, and bogs are all wetlands. For a long time, wetlands were thought to have no value, but now we know that they are among the most important areas on the earth.

THE IMPORTANCE OF WETLANDS

- Wetlands are feeding, breeding, and nursery areas for fish and shellfish.

- Wetlands are home for a third of the United States' resident bird species and half of the migrating birds.

- Wetlands lock up large amounts of carbon in the form of peat, thus preventing it from entering our atmosphere as carbon dioxide, which would contribute to global warming.

- Wetlands absorb and filter out pollutants that would otherwise make our rivers, lakes, and reservoirs unhealthy.

- Wetlands are the glue that holds the land together. They protect the coast and inland areas from too much water in the wrong place at the wrong time. They hold or sponge up water from storms and floods.

THE WETLANDS CAFETERIA

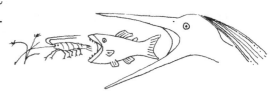

- "Eat and be eaten." In the coastal salt marshes, shrimp eat the smooth cord-grass. The shrimp are eaten by fish. Birds, such as herons, eat the fish. This is called the food chain.

THE GIANTS OF WETLANDS

- Canada has 25 percent of the world's wetlands. 70 percent of the United State's wetlands are found in Alaska. Wetlands are the major destination of all the important flying routes of waterfowl.

Things That You Can Do

- Join local and national conservation groups (page 101).

- Join summer programs about our water world (page 102).

- Learn about careers in conservation, marine science, etc. (page 100).

- Use only environmentally friendly chemical products.

- Conserve water

- Don't use pesticides on your lawn. Develop a wildflower or prairie-grass meadow. This invites butterflies and birds.

- If you have stories to write in school, or other projects, pick an issue that involves the survival of an animal or of our water world.

- Don't teach your trash to swim. Plastics are the most common pollution in the ocean. Plastic kills seals and birds. They think it is fish. Sea turtles think it is a jellyfish. It can block the digestive tract. Cut the plastic rings that hold cans together. These can strangle birds and other animals.

- Form groups with friends, parents, and teachers to identify and publicize local polluters and other dangers to our world. Be brave and strong. It is your future.

Our earth looks like a blue jewel in the blackness of the universe. The blue color is our precious water world. We must protect this jewel and all its inhabitants.

Careers in Marine Science

There are many ways that you can pursue your interest in marine science.

Aquarists: Maintain the aquatic exhibits at aquariums.

Aquatic veterinarians: Work with marine mammals, work in fish farming, treat pet fish, work in basic fish and marine mammal investigation.

Marine biologists: Study plants and animals in the marine world.

Oceanographers: Study the chemistry, geology, and other physical properties of the ocean.

Oceanographic engineers: Design and build instruments and vehicles for studying the ocean.

Underwater filmmakers: Make films about the marine environment.

Veterinary technicians: Help veterinarians care for fish and marine mammals.

To find out more about training or experience in marine careers write to:

American Association of Zoological Parks
  and Aquariums
Oglebay Park
Wheeling, WV 26003

International Oceanographic Foundation
10 Rickenbacker Causeway, Virginia Key
Miami, FL 33149

Conservation and Education Organizations

··

American Cetacean Society
PO Box 4416
San Pedro, CA 90731

Center for Environmental Education
624 9th St. NW
Washington, DC 20001

Center for Marine Conservation
1725 DeSales St. NW, Suite 500
Washington, DC 20036

Cetacean Society International
190 Stillwold Dr.
Wethersfield, CT 06109

Cousteau Society
930 W. 21st St.
Norfolk, VA 23517

Ducks Unlimited
One Waterfowl Way
Long Grove, IL 60047

AquaVet
University of Pennsylvania Veterinary
  School
3800 Spruce Street
Philadelphia, PA 19104

Or talk to staff members at the aquariums or marine science programs at colleges and universities.

Greenpeace U.S.A.
1436 U St. NW
Washington, DC 20009

Izaak Walton League of America
1401 Wilson Blvd., Level B
Arlington, VA 22209

National Audubon Society
PO Box 52529
Boulder, CO 80322

National Geographic Society
Educational Services, Dept. 89
1145 17th Street, NW
Washington, DC 20036

National Wildlife Federation
1400 16th St. NW
Washington, DC 20036-2266

Nature Conservancy
1800 N. Kent St.
Arlington, VA 22209

Padilla Bay National Estuarine
  Research Reserve
1043 Bayview-Edison Rd.
Mount Vernon, WA 98273

Save the Manatee Club
500 N. Maitland Ave.
Maitland, FL 32751

Wetlands Institute
1075 Stone Harbor Blvd.
Stone Harbor, NJ 08247-1424

World Wildlife Fund
1319 18th St. NW
Washington, DC 20036

Summer Opportunities

Coastal Experience
Wilderness Southeast
711 Sandtown Rd.
Savannah, GA 31410

Marine Science Center
17771 Fjord Dr. NE
Poulsbo, WA 98370

Mariner Programs
Mystic Seaport Museum, Dept. 323
Mystic, CT 06355

Ocean Research and Education Society
19 Harbor Loop
Gloucester, MA 01930

Pre-College Summer Programs
Marine Science Consortium, Inc.
PO Box 16
Enterprise St.
Wallops Island, VA 23337

Sea Camp *or* Sail Camp
San Francisco Bay Oceanic Society
Fort Mason Center, Bldg. E
San Francisco, CA 94123

Publications

Ocean Realm Magazine
342 W. Sunset Rd.
San Antonio, TX 78209

Oceans Magazine
2001 W. Main St.
Stamford, CT 06902

Oceanus Magazine
Woods Hole Oceanographic Institute
Woods Hole, MA 02543

Sea Frontiers Magazine
308 West Hitt St.
Mount Morris, IL 61054-8003

World Magazine
National Geographic
PO Box 2330
Washington, DC 20013-2330

More information and publications are available at:

- Aquariums and oceanariums.

- Marine science and oceanography departments of colleges and universities.

- State departments of marine sciences.

- Sea grant programs.

INDEX
. . . .